LIVERPOOL
the Port and its Ships

LIVERPOOL
the Port and its Ships

Michael Stammers

ALAN SUTTON

First published in the United Kingdom in 1991
Alan Sutton Publishing Ltd · Phoenix Mill · Far Thrupp · Stroud
Gloucestershire

First published in the United States of America in 1991
Alan Sutton Publishing Inc · Wolfeboro Falls · NH 03896–0848

British Library Cataloguing in Publication Data

Stammers, M.K. (Michael K.)
  Liverpool, the port and its ships.
  1. Merseyside (Metropolitan County). Liverpool. Ports:
  Port of Liverpool, history
  I. Title
  387.10942753   PPR   05172266

  ISBN 0–86299–728–3

Library of Congress Cataloging in Publication Data

Stammers, Michael.
  Liverpool, the port and its ships / Michael Stammers.
    p.   cm.
  ISBN 0-86299-728-3
  1. Liverpool (England—Description—Views. 2. Harbors–
England—Liverpool—History—Pictorial works. 3. Ships—
England—Liverpool—History—Pictorial works. I. Title.
  DA690.L8S66 1991
  942.7′53—dc20   91–17246
                                                        CIP

Cover illustration: Liverpool, past and present. *Alexandra Towing Company;* inset
David Smith Collection, Liverpool Nautical Research Society.

Typeset in 11/14 Palatino.
Typesetting and origination by Alan Sutton Publishing Limited.
Printed in Great Britain by WBC Print Limited, Bridgend, Wales.

CONTENTS

ACKNOWLEDGEMENTS   6

Chapter One   THE RIVER AND THE CITY   7

Chapter Two   THE DOCKS   30

Chapter Three   DEEP-SEA SAILING SHIPS   49

Chapter Four   FISHING   62

Chapter Five   LINERS   69

Chapter Six   COASTERS, FERRIES AND TUGS   89

Chapter Seven   YACHTS AND PADDLERS   108

Chapter Eight   LIGHTHOUSES, LIGHTSHIPS
                 AND SERVICE VESSELS   117

Chapter Nine   COASTAL SCHOONERS   128

Chapter Ten   THE ROYAL NAVY   141

Chapter Eleven   TANKERS AND CONTAINER
                 SHIPS   152

ACKNOWLEDGEMENTS

I would like to thank the following for their kind permission to reproduce the large number of black and white photographs: Alexandra Towing Company; The Bath Marine Museum; David Smith Collection, Liverpool Nautical Research Society; Liverpool City Engineers; Mersey Docks and Harbour Company; Trustees of NMGM including Stewart Bale, Williams Collection, and Mersey Docks and Harbour Board Collection.

Chapter One

THE RIVER AND THE CITY

This collection of photographs illustrates the history of the port of Liverpool both at its peak in 1850–1914 and in its decline in the later part of this century. Liverpool was a port of world renown. Sailors told stories of its pubs and girls. It was the 'liner port' *par excellence* with cargo and passenger liners plying to every continent. It was the biggest exporting port of the United Kingdom at a time when our country dominated the manufacture of every kind of factory-made product and it was the second biggest importer following very closely after London. Liverpool was the second city of the British Empire and its shipowners and merchants controlled millions of pounds of assets and millions of tons of shipping. Indeed, in 1900, Liverpool-registered ships accounted for almost a tenth of the world's ships. It was a great crossroads of sea and land; distributing goods was its business, not manufacturing.

Today it can make no such claims. It is still a considerable port, with some twenty million tons of traffic. But much of this is moved in great single parcels by oil tankers or container ships. The docks seem empty in comparison with earlier times, and many of the smaller, less useful ones, especially those to the south of the Pier Head, have been filled in or converted to new uses. Young people learn to sail dinghies where the Booth Liners, going a thousand miles up the Amazon, and the steamers of MacAndrews for Spain and Portugal once berthed. The Albert Dock once accommodated tiers of wooden sailing ships, discharging rum, tobacco, cotton and sugar; its vaults and chambers now house shops, flats, offices, museums and art galleries.

The reasons for the changes were varied and complex. Increased competition for cargo and passenger traffic was one factor. The building of the Manchester Ship Canal which opened in 1894 diverted traffic from Liverpool. The rivalry for emigrants and passengers with Hamburg and Southampton grew in the same decade. The great liners such as White Star and Cunard moved their main services down south to Southampton. It was nearer London and there were no difficult approaches to an enclosed dock system. More recently, the competition from jet aircraft killed the remainder of the long-distance passenger trade. The shifting pattern of trade, particularly the increase in business with our Common Market partners, has given traffic to east coast competitors. The containerization of deep-sea trades has meant that services have often been concentrated at one port. It is easier to move containers by road or rail than make several stops with a large container ship. In the late sixties, for example, all Liverpool's Far East liner business was merged into a new consortium – Ocean Container Liners – who chose Southampton as their British terminal. There have been labour troubles and a lack of investment in new facilities. The port authority, the Mersey Docks and Harbour Board founded in 1858, was not always as flexible and as far-seeing as it should have been. Not all of the dock facilities built were a success. The shipowners suffered tremendous losses through enemy action in two world wars and in the second, the port itself – so crucial to the war effort – was terribly damaged by enemy bombers.

This then is some of the background to the photographs. The other essential background fact is the character of the River Mersey. This has three parts: a wide outer estuary, Liverpool Bay, a narrow middle section where Liverpool stands and a wider, shallower upper estuary that finishes some twenty miles inland at Warrington. The narrow middle section creates a 'venturi' effect with the waters of the river. Tides can sweep through it at up to seven or eight miles an hour. The difference between high and low tide can be as much as ten metres (thirty feet). The sand and silt from the upper estuary is carried in suspension by the fast flowing tide. As it comes to the wider outer estuary, the current slows down and the suspended grains are deposited on the river bed. This creates numerous banks and bars in the approaches to the port. Before the days of the specially built training banks the approach channels could move dramatically over a matter of months. It was therefore a difficult port to enter and once inside the rise and fall of the tide made it awkward to unload. On the other hand, it was strategically placed to handle the exports of Lancashire and Cheshire cloth, coal and salt, and despite all the physical difficulties of the river, the port of Liverpool grew and grew in the eighteenth and nineteenth centuries.

Liverpool began to trade deep-sea in the second half of the seventeenth century. The growth of the port was the enterprise of its merchants and sea captains who were rewarded by a growing share of the trade to the colonies in North America and the West Indies. Money was raised to build a dock (opened in 1715) and to canalize local rivers to improve distribution to the hinterland. It grew wealthy and notorious on its part in the supply of African labour for the West Indian plantations. Thousands of negroes were transported, crammed tight in Liverpool ships, to slave at producing crops of sugar cane, tobacco and cotton. The slave trade when abolished in 1807 witnessed a wider diversification of trading to South America for example and to China and India. By 1850, and the first generation of photographers, it had grown beyond all expectation, a huge commercial magnet drawing in ships and people from all parts of the world, attracting the poor emigrant in search of a better life away from the land and the thrusting entrepreneur bent on making his fortune in cotton, ships or merchandise.

Low tide on the Mersey about 1860. Note the bathing machines on the
New Brighton shore.

Trustees of NMGM

High tide, an Esso tanker inward bound. The effects of sunlight and
cloud on the muddy waters of the Mersey can often be magical.

Williams Collection, Trustees of NMGM

The incoming tide at Egremont ferry about 1914. As the ferry departs for the Liverpool landing stage, a White Star liner slips down the river and out to sea bound for New York.

Trustees of NMGM

The river and the city were dominated by the docks. Liverpool's North Docks stretched from Gladstone Dock, under construction at bottom left, upriver to Canada Dock. This is one of the earliest aerial photographs of the port taken about 1924/25.

Liverpool City Engineers

St Nicholas Church, though much rebuilt, represents continuity with Liverpool's medieval past. The original ships of the town would land on the beach below its dominant tower. By 1870 it was surrounded by office buildings and warehouses with the eighteenth-century George's Basin between it and the river.

Stewart Bale, Trustees of NMGM

The Mersey is more like an inland sea than an ordinary river estuary.
An Alexandra tug sails out to meet an inward bound cargo liner.

The city was a place of contrasts of squalor and luxury, of very wealthy
and very poor. Exchange Flags behind the Town Hall was the regular
meeting place for the cotton brokers, merchants and shipowners of the
town to do deals and exchange gossip. Top hats and tail coats were the
essential uniform.

The dock road was a place of continuous motion, horse buses, carts and team wagons constantly shifting goods to and from the quaysides. Warehouse to ship's hold. This is George's Dock about 1860. Note the number of ships tied up alongside the low transit shed and the Goree warehouses.

The Bath Marine Museum

The Pier Head and the Landing Stage for the ferries and liners was the heart of the city. This was especially so after the construction of the three large office buildings on the site of George's Dock and George's Dock Basin. From left to right they are the Liver Building (1911), Cunard Building (1916), Mersey Docks and Harbour Board Building (1907). On the right hand side the small dock is the Manchester Dock once used to provide a barge service between Liverpool and Manchester via the canalized Rivers Mersey and Irwell.

Liverpool City Engineers

Many people both from Britain and Europe came to Liverpool in transit for a better life abroad. North America and Australia were particularly popular destinations. The great liner companies relied on the immigrants as a stable cargo and organized hostels and transport for them. This photograph shows immigrants about to depart by horse bus for the Cunard liner *Lucania*.

Trustees of NMGM

Casual labour often on a half day basis was the norm in many of the port industries particularly for dock and transport workers. The town also attracted many poor immigrants from Ireland and other parts of England, Scotland and Wales.

Williams Collection,
Trustees of NMGM

The Liverpool Landing Stage, now alas scrapped and replaced by a concrete successor, was once the longest floating structure in the world. It was the terminal for the great passenger liners as well as the ferries. It witnessed the departure of millions of people, both the famous and the first class, and the poor steerage immigrants. This picture shows the departure of the White Star liner *Celtic* on 2 June 1923.

MDHB Collection, Trustees of NMGM

Besides the immigrants, there was a huge population of seafarers in transit in Liverpool and a whole leisure industry grew up to cater for their needs. 'Sailortown' was a notorious aspect of Liverpool life and many inward bound seafarers with the accumulated wages of months were ripped off. The Seaman's Home founded in 1846 was designed to provide reasonable lodgings for the transient seafarer.

Bath Marine Museum

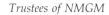

Unfortunately, the cast iron interior had the atmosphere of a Victorian jail.

A cabin for the Seaman's Home. To quote an old seafarer who stayed there: 'This looks like two young teetotallers turning in, for there are no bottles or papers of fish and chips on the table. Neither have they turned out their pockets of tobacco and matches or loose change on the table – always a necessary preamble prior to undressing.'

Railway lines and railway buildings were as big a feature of the port as the ships and the quays. They were an essential part of the distribution system that moved cargoes to and from the ships. The Great Western Railway depot at Manchester Dock was unusual because it had no railway lines. The company's nearest railhead to Liverpool was at Birkenhead and the final passage into Liverpool was by barges into Manchester Dock. The lightship *Planet* in the foreground is in Canning Number 2 Graving Dock.

Trustees of NMGM

The dock railway near Wapping Dock in 1958. A dock shunting engine known as a 'Pug' draws past and above is the Overhead railway. This was closed in 1957 and as can be seen in the picture was being dismantled.

Trustees of NMGM

Shipbuilding was a major local industry. The shipyards on the Liverpool side of the river were gradually closed down to make way for dock extensions and the last major shipyard finished in the South Docks in 1899. Laird's, later Cammell Laird's yard, continued to flourish on the Birkenhead side. It had been a pioneer of iron shipbuilding and this view between 1860 and 1870 shows the scale and complexity of the yard with four ships in dry dock and five under construction.

Trustees of NMGM

Ship repair was another vital service. The Customs launch *Vulcan* and a Mersey light buoy undergo painting in Canning Number 1 Graving Dock about 1950.

Sugar was one of the first oceanic imports into Liverpool. This spectacular warehouse was completed about 1958 to house sugar in bulk.

Wines and spirits
including rum were
also large-scale imports
and there were many
bonded warehouses
rich with smells
emanating from the
casks in store.

Trustees of NMGM

As the city expanded,
the better off moved to
cleaner, greener
suburbs on the
outskirts or across the
river on the Wirral.
Mingled with the
warehouses and
factories, crowded,
squalid slums housed
a vast population of
working people.
Multiple occupation,
overcrowding, disease,
lack of water and
sanitary facilities were
all insidious features of
Liverpool life.

Trustees of NMGM

Much of this imported liquor was bottled in Liverpool for re-export or internal distribution. There were also other important food and drink processing firms and their products ranged from sweets and biscuits to flour, tinned goods and beer.

Trustees of NMGM

The public house was an important institution. Many had nautical connections such as Walker's 'Neptune'. Sir Andrew Barclay Walker gave the city its splendid Walker Art Gallery in 1873.

Stewart Bale Collection, Trustees of NMGM

Another Liverpool pub with a nautical connection. Above the radiator hangs a splendid oil painting of a Cunard liner by Samuel Walters, the leading marine artist of mid-nineteenth-century Liverpool. Liverpool people took great pride in their ships whether they were shipowners, seafarers or other citizens.

Stewart Bale Collection, Trustees of NMGM

Chapter Two

THE DOCKS

From the Gladstone Dock at the northern end of Liverpool to the Herculaneum Dock at the south of the River Mersey, Liverpool was fronted for a length of $6\frac{1}{2}$ miles by a system of docks and basins with a water area of 458 acres and 27 miles of quays. There were docks of every imaginable type and variety, capable of accommodating both coasters and Atlantic liners. On the opposite bank of the river there were the Birkenhead Docks with 182 acres of water and 9 miles of quays. In other words, the dock estate was vast. It was also cut off from the town and the rest of the world by high defensive walls, pierced at intervals by sliding gates protected by dock policemen on sentry duty. From 1858, docks on both sides of the Mersey were governed by the Mersey Docks and Harbour Board. The members of this body were elected from port users such as shipowners together with representatives from the government bodies such as the Board of Trade and the Mersey Conservancy Commission. It was very much a law unto itself so far as affairs in the estate were concerned and it controlled a large staff of clerks, dock gatemen and construction crews to run and maintain the port. It ran a fleet of maintenance and specialist ships such as dredgers and floating cranes, and it possessed acres of floorspace in warehouses to store all incoming cargoes, which included anything from elephant tusks to finest cognac. In addition to its own staff, an army of dock workers – stevedores, tally clerks, porters – were casually employed by cargo handling firms to load and discharge the ships. The board charged dues for the use of the docks and its facilities and it could borrow money by Act of Parliament to raise capital to build new docks. Its engineers such as Jesse Hartley (1824–1860) and his successors built soundly and with an eye to the future. The Victorian docks have survived the constant surge of the Mersey. Latterly they also built large and deep so that the North Docks such as the Gladstone, opened in 1927, can still serve modern ships. Its final project, the building of a giant new dock – the Royal Seaforth – in the early seventies proved too much. This was a multi-purpose dock with a new grain terminal and container base capable of accepting ships of up to 70,000 tons. At a time of falling revenues, it proved too expensive and the board had to be reconstituted with government help as the Mersey Docks and Harbour Company. The company has continued the work of re-shaping and modernizing the working docks, while many of the obsolete smaller docks have been transferred to the government sponsored Merseyside Development Corporation for redevelopment for non-port uses.

The docks have lock-gates at their entrances so that the water within can be retained as the tide goes out in the river. The ships within therefore remain safely afloat. Early on, a threshold or foyer dock was arranged so that the sailing ships could take down their sails before being winched by capstans into the dock itself. These developed into a series of 'half-tide basins' which acted as holding areas for ships entering and leaving while the water in the river crept level with the water inside the dock. In the mid-twentieth century, double locks were built to replace the half-tide system at Gladstone, Langton, Waterloo, Brunswick and Birkenhead entrances. This allows a vessel the possibility of entering the docks whatever the state of the tide rather than two or less hours before high water. In actuality, most ship movements still take place on or around high tide. The docks were Liverpool and Liverpool was the docks and in their heyday they attracted both popular and professional attention. They were tourist attractions as far back as 1796 when the first 'strangers' guide to Liverpool was published and the French writer, Hippolyte Taine, wrote in the 1860s: 'But the appearance of the docks dominates all. The Mersey is broad as a channel of the sea, opens outwards to the west, bearing ships inwards and outwards. Along its banks for a six-mile length they sail into canals and stone-walled basins like a complicated warren of load and unload. Their furled masts seem like a wintry forest, enclosing the horizon to the north . . . the sight, I think, is one of the most splendid in the world.'

Mersey Docks and Harbour Board founded in 1858 undertook an almost continuous programme of building new docks and improving existing ones. The scale of the civil engineering works involved can be readily appreciated from the photograph which shows the reconstruction of Brunswick Dock in 1907. The old dry docks are being replaced with a concrete quay to provide additional accommodation for cargo liners, some of which can be seen in the background.

MDHB Collection, Trustees of NMGM

Each dock entrance was fitted with massive lock-gates fashioned from long-lasting tropical timbers such as greenheart. They penned the water inside the docks as the tide fell so that ships could stay afloat and out of danger. The maintenance and staffing of the dock gates was a major item in the Dock Board's budget. It also built large public warehouses and the ones in this picture at Waterloo Dock were designed to store grain in bulk.

Bath Marine Museum

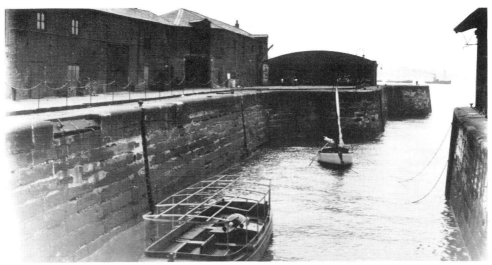

Tidal inlets like Chester Basin at the Pier Head were reminders that Liverpool's first trading vessels were simply ditched on the foreshore in front of the town. These ferry basins were used by nineteenth-century ferries until the construction of the landing stages. Chester Basin had no lock-gates and dried out at low tide.

MDHB Collection, Trustees of NMGM

Much of the river wall on the Liverpool side was constructed by the dock engineer, Jesse Hartley (1824–1860), who used a random style of large and small blocks which was called cyclopean masonry. He also built houses at the dock entrances to accommodate the dock masters and their families.

Trustees of NMGM

The Dock Masters office at Clarence Dock. Another characteristically eccentric piece of Hartley architecture. Clarence Dock was opened in 1830 as a special dock to segregate steamers from the rest of the wooden sailing ships of the port.

MDHB Collection, Trustees of NMGM

Hartley built large bonded warehouses on the quayside into which vessels could discharge valuable cargoes directly. This is the Wapping Warehouse in about 1865 with a brigantine and three Mersey flats alongside.

Bath Marine Museum

These huge steam engines at Huskisson Dock lying derelict in the photograph were used to increase the depth of water in the docks in order to cope with the increasing size of ships in the late nineteenth century.

Trustees of NMGM

Transit sheds were used to protect cargo coming on and off a ship and as sorting and weighing areas. A vast range of packages, barrels, boxes and bales were all delivered on the landward side. All had to be accounted for and loaded in the correct position in the ship's hold. It was a complex and time consuming business. Major shipping companies rented particular quays for their own use. This picture was taken at Kings Dock probably at the Booth Line's berth in the mid-1930s.

MDHB Collection, Trustees of NMGM

The Blue Funnel Line's berth at Gladstone Dock (opened in 1927) represented the most modern cargo handling practice with a wide quay available for rail and road traffic, mobile electric cranes and a three storey reinforced concrete transit shed behind. This photograph was taken in 1956.

Trustees of NMGM

Barrels were the universal container of the nineteenth century. Anything liquid or dry would be packed inside them for transport abroad.
This is George's Dock West Quay in about 1870. Note also the Windsor
Foundry's substantially built wagon for transporting pieces of iron
work.

Bath Marine Museum

Demand for barrels was so great that several hundred coopers were
employed in making and repairing them in Liverpool. Today the craft is
still perpetuated in an original cooperage at Albert Dock as part of the
Maritime Museum.

Trustees of NMGM

Liverpool was a pioneer of motor road transport. This picture shows
the Vauxhall warehousing company's premises at Albert Dock in the
1950s.

Trustees of NMGM

Liverpool was the leading export port of the United Kingdom. It drew much of its custom from the industries of the North West and the Midlands.

Stewart Bale, Trustees of NMGM

Virtually every package, barrel and bale had to be man-handled. Although dock work was on a casual basis, it called for a wide range of skills in slinging the cargo, loading and packing it in the ship's hold to ensure that it was safe and stable on the voyage.

Stewart Bale, Trustees of NMGM

Cargoes could be as diverse as Lancashire cottons to huge steam engines built by the Vulcan foundry of Newton-le-Willows for Indian railways. This picture shows locomotives being loaded at Birkenhead about 1936.

Trustees of NMGM

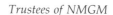

The Mersey Docks were not confined within the boundaries of Liverpool. The later North Docks spread across into the neighbouring borough of Bootle, and to the south the London and North Western Railway built a rival port at Garston. The docks at Birkenhead had also originally been built to compete with Liverpool but were joined with them under the new Mersey Docks and Harbour Board in 1858. Garston specialized in coal exports especially to Ireland and this photograph shows the coal tips.

Liverpool City Engineers

Discharging boxes of apples from a Dutch coaster in Albert Dock.

Trustees of NMGM

The same scene from the quayside. The tally man is sitting checking off the number of boxes while the customs official looks on.

Trustees of NMGM

Some cargoes had special quays or docks solely to handle them. Timber was a major import particularly from North America, and the Brunswick Dock (1834) and Canada Dock (1858) were intended for the discharge of timber from sailing vessels. Large lengths of timber were unloaded through openings in the bows of the vessels. They were dragged ashore either by teams of men or horses and this animated scene at Canada Dock is depicted in one of the paintings that adorn the offices of the Mersey Docks and Harbour Board.

MDHB Collection, Trustees of NMGM

Liverpool became one of the major grain importing ports for Britain. In the second half of the nineteenth century our own agricultural industry could not grow enough food for the booming urban population and large quantities of grain, meat and other foodstuff were imported from Canada, United States, Argentina, Australia and New Zealand. Grain, because of its low value, was considered a bulk commodity to be carried in sailing ships. However, the sailing ships' position in the grain trade was rapidly eroded by an increasing number of economical tramp steamers that carried grain in bulk rather than in sacks. Specialist grain handling facilities existed on both sides of the river.

Trustees of NMGM

The Mersey Docks and Harbour Board were a major employer in the port and they had a wide-ranging workforce from specialist craftsmen building dock gates to clerks in the engineer's drawing office. They maintained large maintenance depots for the upkeep of the port. The biggest was at Coburg dockyard where several hundred men were employed. This picture shows the weekly pay day outside the dockyard on 1 November 1902. The social distinction between the clerical staff with their bowler hats and the rest of the workforce can be clearly seen.

MDHB Collection, Trustees of NMGM

The Port of Liverpool came under increasing competition from other United Kingdom and continental ports at the end of the nineteenth century. Its position was further eroded after the First World War by the loss of traffic, the general decline of British industry and the catastrophic world recession that was ushered in by the great collapse of 1929. Parts of the docks were put over to new uses or remodelled. For example, the Clarence Dock, once the centre of steam traffic, was transformed into the Clarence Dock power station and the surrounding docks modernized to accommodate the Coast Lines' ships. This aerial photograph was taken about 1955.

Trustees of NMGM

In 1971 the whole of the South Dock system was closed to traffic. In the space of ten years the docks which were opened to the river silted up rapidly and vegetation overran the quaysides. This picture at Canning Dock shows this and also the new modern office blocks that were put up on the site of the first dock in Liverpool opened in 1715.

Trustees of NMGM

The potential of these abandoned South Docks was first demonstrated when the Merseyside County Council opened a pilot phase of the Maritime Museum in 1980 at Canning Dock. This shows the dry docks put to new use with the Liverpool pilot boat *Edmund Gardner* preserved in one dock and a wide selection of smaller craft including Sir Alec Rose's *Lively Lady* in the other.

Trustees of NMGM

Chapter Three

DEEP-SEA SAILING SHIPS

Liverpool's first deep-sea sailing ships go back to the seventeenth century when the first tentative trading voyages by local vessels to West Africa, the West Indies and North America got under way. The vessels were small wooden full-rigged ships averaging about 200 tons. They gradually increased in size but retained the same rig well into the nineteenth century.

The 'Clipper' ship, a radical new design of fast sailing deep-sea ships, was developed in the 1840s, and vessels of this type were brought by Liverpool firms particularly for trades with high paying freights requiring speedy delivery, such as the tea trade from China, and the emigration trade to Australia after the discovery of gold in New South Wales in 1851. The large wooden American-built three-masted sailing ships of Liverpool's Black Ball Line and White Star Line set new records for the passage out to Australia.

Much ocean carrying was still conducted in vessels of quite small size: brigs and three-masted barques of 200 to 300 tons were very common traders to the west coast of South America, which involved the worst passage in the world round Cape Horn in both directions; for example, the *Jhelum*, a ship of 427 tons, built at Liverpool in 1949 and owned by Steel and Co. of Liverpool, was a regular trader to the west coast, for cargoes of copper ore and guano until 1870 when she was abandoned in Stanley in the Falkland Islands. She is still lying there as a mastless hulk – the last Liverpool wooden sailing ship.

The high freight trades and liner trades were all gradually taken over by steam vessels. Even at the generally recognized peak of sailing ship development, steam ships were having an impact on the North Atlantic routes; for example in 1854 the Inman Steamship Company started the carriage of steerage of passengers to North America for the first time. But the sailing ships remained supreme on the long-distance routes so long as steamships were handicapped by lack of coaling stations and heavy coal consumption. The development of compact, economical compound engines meant that the end of the sailing ship monopoly was inevitable, and in the last three decades the general trend was the development of large iron (and later steel) bulk carrying sail-vessels designed for maximum economy rather than speed. Most vessels were in the tramp trades picking up cargoes as they were offered. The trade crystallized into fairly well-defined patterns, for example coal from England and South Australia to the west coast of South America, grain from the west coast of North America and Australia to Europe, nitrates and guano from the west coast of South America to Europe. Sailing vessels faced increasing competition from growing fleets of cargo steamers even in these trades and the strictest economies were necessary to make any profits.

The four-masted barque rig was adopted in favour of the ship rig for vessels of over 2,000 tons because it could be worked by smaller crews. From the late 1890s, culminating in the years 1908 to 1910, there was a steady sale of Liverpool sailing ships to foreign owners as trading conditions worsened. Some owners re-invested in steam ships. Many retired from business.

The surviving owners carried on only by the strictest, most niggardly economies; ships' crews were reduced to dangerously small numbers, often with a large proportion of apprentices; sails, food and all stores were strictly rationed. Many vessels became sitting targets for German submarines in the First World War. The tall masts of sailing ships had a tremendous visual impact on the port of Liverpool, towering above sheds and warehouses. But after 1914 these beautiful vessels became rare sights in the port. Scandinavian-owned barques delivered Australian grain until 1939 and after that the visit of a training ship was the only opportunity to see a big sailing ship in the port.

George's Dock about 1865. From left to right: a small iron full-rigged ship, a topsail schooner and a brig.

Bath Marine Museum

George's Dock about 1897/98 with two iron three-masted barques. Note the background with the bridge of the Overhead railway to the left, the Mersey railway pumping station and the salt warehouses of Mann Island.

Trustees of NMGM

Salthouse Dock in 1907 shows how, at the end of the nineteenth century, the sailing ship had been confined to the smaller docks. The large vessel in the centre of the picture is the four-masted ship *The Highfields*, built in 1892 for C. W. Kellock & Company of Liverpool. With a gross tonnage of 2,280 tons she was one of the largest sailing vessels to use the Salthouse Dock.

Trustees of NMGM

This picture shows Salthouse Dock between 1880 and 1890. It conveys something of the crowded atmosphere of the sailing ship docks with closely-packed ships loading cargo from the quay and out of Mersey flats.

Trustees of NMGM

This photograph shows the former tea clipper *Cutty Sark* in the West Float, Birkenhead, in 1914 when delivering a cargo of whale oil under the Portuguese flag.

MDHB Collection, Trustees of NMGM

Before steam towage was available, ships had to make their own way in the river under sail. This caused frequent damage, delays and disasters. The steam tugs often doubled up as ferries. This painting shows the Liverpool ship *Helen* of 1841 at the entrance to the Mersey, New Brighton. This ship portrait is a reminder of the pride that owners and masters took in their sailing ships. Paintings were still being commissioned in Liverpool long after photography was widely available.

Trustees of NMGM

The *Waterwitch*, under sail in
the river in the early 1930s, was
the last square-rigged British
sailing vessel to trade
commercially.

*David Smith Collection, Liverpool
Nautical Research Society*

Fruit schooners in George's Dock about 1880. Small wooden sailing
vessels of between 100 and 200 tons cargo capacity were employed in
some specialist deep-sea trade up until the First World War.

Trustees of NMGM

There were very few deep-sea sailing vessels in the port after the First World War except for the occasional Scandinavian-owned bulk carrier delivering grain. The value of sailing ships for training seamen was not forgotten and there has been a steady flow of purpose-built sail training ships on courtesy visits to the port. This is the Polish ship *Dar Pomorza* docking at Birkenhead in 1948.

Alexandra Towing Company

Canning Half-Tide Dock about 1875 with an American-built barque tied up alongside the Albert Dock warehouses. The domed building is the Liverpool Customs House.

Trustees of NMGM

One hundred years later, this is the same warehouse but it has been converted into the Merseyside Maritime Museum. The ship alongside is the Danish sail training vessel *Georg Stage* which took part in the Tall Ships Race to Liverpool in 1984.

Trustees of NMGM

This model of a 'Blackwall frigate' is one of the reminders of Liverpool's sailing ship heritage displayed by the Maritime Museum.

Trustees of NMGM

Jhelum is the last surviving example of a Liverpool-built wooden sailing ship. Built in 1849 she was abandoned in Port Stanley, Falkland Islands, in 1871.

Trustees of NMGM

Jhelum again, bow
view.

Prince's Dock, full of deep-sea square riggers about 1890.

Four-masted barque *Benares* in Canning Half-Tide Dock about 1910.

Trustees of NMGM

Chapter Four

FISHING

Liverpool was never a very important fishing station, although a small fleet of fishing boats served to supply the local market; in the latter half of the eighteenth century, there was also an attempt to take part in the Arctic whaling expeditions.

By the 1870s, two distinct types of local fishing boat had developed: ketch rigged trawlers of about 38 to 40 tons of which there were thirty-five registered at Liverpool in 1872 and cutter-rigged inshore boats, nicknamed 'nobbies' which mainly trawled for shrimps for the seaside resort markets of Southport and New Brighton.

The big trawlers were mainly owned and manned by the Wirral village of Hoylake; but they usually landed their catches at Canning Dock, Liverpool. Their main fishing grounds were in Liverpool Bay, but some boats worked as far south as Cardigan Bay, where there was a rich inshore ground off Aberystwth. The crew numbered four men and a boy and were usually away between five and six days. The trawl, mostly sole, cod, plaice, haddock and roker, was hand-hauled aboard by a winch until the introduction of steam capstans in the 1890s.

In 1889, four steam trawlers arrived in Liverpool, owned by the Liverpool Steam Trawling Company; by 1900 there was a fleet of about sixteen steam trawlers based on Canning Dock. With the increasing pollution and rising costs, the last company in the business, Harley & Miller Limited, stopped fishing in 1939.

The inshore boats (the nobbies) were based at several different places on the river and along the coast, as far inland as Runcorn, and as far north as Southport. They were yacht-like, thirty-foot, half-decked cutters, very similar to the Morecambe Bay nobbies. They fished on a daily basis for shrimps or sole usually with a crew of two. As many as seventy boats would work in the Southport area at the height of the shrimping season between August and November. A good day's catch would amount to about thirty quarts of shrimps and immediately they were caught these were usually boiled in a smaller boiler fitted in the shallow cockpit. The Southport grounds became increasingly difficult to work after 1900 because of silting; but a few boats (often with auxiliary engines) continued to work out of the Mersey. Today, although there are hardly any full-time inshore fishermen, the nobbies have been resuscitated by enthusiastic sailors who have rebuilt them and restored them to their original lofty rig. The annual nobby race on the Mersey is one of the great summer spectacles of Liverpool. A handful of foreign beam trawlers are also based in the port.

This shows two sailing trawlers in Albert Dock. Fish catches were normally landed in nearby Canning Dock and ice was taken on board in Albert Dock from the refrigerated store set up in D Warehouse in 1899.

Williams Collection, Trustees of NMGM

Sailing trawler outward bound. These local craft were owned and manned by the fishermen of Hoylake. Their main fishing ground was off the Isle of Man and each trip lasted about a week.

Trustees of NMGM

No trawlers have survived but the remains of the *Emblematic* which was wrecked near Hoylake and subsequently embedded in the sea wall were retrieved in 1977 and recorded.

Trustees of NMGM

The cockle woman suggests something of the hardships of life in the fishing communities at the mouth of the estuary. Although this photograph has always been known as the 'cockle woman', she appears to be gathering a larger type of shellfish.

Williams Collection, Trustees of NMGM

Unloading the catch from two of Harley & Miller's steam trawlers at Canning Dock about 1935.

Trustees of NMGM

Nobbies under sail in
Liverpool Bay.

Dr Dennis Chapman

Repairing a nobby at Rock Ferry. Note HMS *Conway* in the background.

Dr Dennis Chapman

Returning with the catch.

Chapter Five

LINERS

Steamers offered the possibility of regular 'liner' services for ocean voyages, and the late 1830s marked the start of the transatlantic service by steamers. The early steamers were all paddlers powered by bulky side-lever engines, worked on low pressure steam from crude boilers. Much of the hull space was taken up by machinery and bunkers so that they were scarcely profitable without high fares and subsidies for carrying mail. The most successful was Samuel Cunard's line whose first ship steamed the Atlantic in 1840. Atlantic liners were well established by the 1850s with promising developments of screw propulsion and iron hulls.

But the progress in engine design was not sufficiently advanced to enable the steamers to compete on the more long-distance routes to Australia and the Far East. There were a number of sailing ships with auxiliary engines and these enjoyed limited success. Liverpool engineer and shipowner, Alfred Holt, designed an economical long-distance cargo liner. He first demonstrated his ideas on a small experimental vessel in 1864 and then put them to the commercial test by ordering three vessels of his own design. The *Agamemnon*, the *Ajax* and the *Achilles* sailed for China in 1866. They had long iron hulls, compound engines of his design, high pressure boilers, and were capable of steaming 8,500 miles to the first coaling station at Mauritius, with 3,000 tons of cargo.

The opening of the Suez Canal in 1869 reduced voyage times by as much as twelve days and gave further advantage to the steamers. The establishment of strategically-sited coaling stations and business agencies in the Far East also contributed much to turning Holt's technical success into a commercial one. By 1870, Liverpool shipowners were running steam liner services from Liverpool to all continents.

However, the North American connection was the most important and prestigious. The competition intensified as new lines such as the National Line in 1863, the Guion Line in 1866 and the White Star Line in 1871 were established. Lines competed by building faster, bigger ships and providing greater comfort for passengers (at least for the first class users). By 1889 the White Star's *Teutonic* (1889) for example had twin screws, no sails, electric lights and could be equipped as a fast cruiser in wartime.

The glamorous image of these sumptuous floating hotels received a profound shock with the sinking of the White Star's *Titanic* in April 1912. Although White Star had been American controlled since 1902 and docked its express liners at Southampton in preference to Liverpool, the *Titanic* was registered in Liverpool and was considered a local ship.

The Cunard Line's *Mauretania* and *Lusitania* (1907) were the most famous of the Liverpool liners. They were the largest vessels of their day, 32,000 tons with steam turbines giving them 75 per cent more power than any previous liners. They beat the German competition with voyages averaging over 25 and 26 knots.

The cargo liners of the Liverpool fleet had also continued to change and progress. From Alfred Holt's innovations onwards, the Liverpool cargo liner had increased in size and numbers; Holts, Harrisons, Booths, Bibbys, Leylands, Lamport & Holt, Elder Dempster and others helped to make Liverpool the biggest exporting port of the United Kingdom. The organization of conferences to agree freight rates for specific trades owed much of their inspiration to Liverpool. These helped to stabilize trades and prevent excessive unprofitable competition.

After 1900, there was a growing number of mergers and take-overs to form larger fleets to meet the competition from subsidized foreign lines and fluctuating trade conditions. However, Liverpool's liner fleet was larger and better equipped than ever before. Cargo liners were built with triple expansion engines carrying twice as much as the 1866 *Agamemnon*. Liners with refrigerated holds delivered meat and fruit to Liverpool from the 1890s. Wireless was standard on the North Atlantic by 1914. The First World War brought chaos; loss of ships through requisition or sinking by the enemy was such that the aftermath was a struggle for survival rather than a struggle for prosperity. Many Liverpool ships rendered distinguished service during the war, notably the armed merchant cruisers. Many fleets needed massive rebuilding and improvement, all in the hope of better times. Cunard, for example, who lost a number of ships including the *Lusitania*, began a programme of modernizing ships by converting them from coal to oil fuel and the building of new ships. Some companies such as Bibbys experimented with motor ships.

The catastrophic worldwide depression from 1929 to 1934 badly affected Liverpool shipping companies. T. & J. Harrisons, who weathered the storm better than most, had laid up fifteen of their fleet of about fifty by 1932, while most of the other vessels maintained a loss-making skeleton service to maintain the company's interest on its

main routes. The worst affected of all the Liverpool
shipping companies were those belonging to Lord
Kylsants' Royal Mail Group, principally Pacific Steam
Navigation Company, Elder Dempster, Glen Line,
Lamport & Holt and the White Star Line. The group
crashed in 1929 leaving the individual companies to find
their own salvation. The White Star Line was merged with
its old rival the Cunard Line in 1934 with assistance from
the government. The government also provided money
for the scrapping of obsolete tonnage and this and the
revival in world trade from 1934 was the beginning of
recovery for Liverpool's steamer fleets until this too was
cut short by the onset of the Second World War. Once
again, Liverpool liners were requisitioned for war service
and suffered huge losses of ships and men. The Blue
Funnel, for example, lost half its fleet of seventy-nine
ships and the small Johnston Warren had five out of six
ships sunk. Most major fleets were rebuilt in the decade
after 1945 but competition was also intensifying. There
was an increasing number of foreign competitors sailing
under cheap 'flags of convenience' or supported by
government subsidy. Many new nationals also wished to
reserve cargo for their own liners too. Jet aircraft provided
a much faster way of travelling and the passenger liners'
services across the Atlantic attracted fewer and fewer
travellers by the mid-1960s. Cunard finished their
Liverpool passenger service in 1967. Canadian Pacific
followed suit in 1971. Conventional cargo liners were
displaced by container ships and roll-on/roll-off vessels. It
was estimated that a large container ship with its easily
stored standard size boxes could do the work of six
ordinary cargo liners. With containerization, services were
concentrated on fewer ports. In 1971 there was a great
blow when what had been Blue Funnel's Far East service

was merged into Overseas Containers Limited with its British calls at Southampton and Tilbury. In fact, the 1970s and '80s have seen a rapid decline in size of the British Merchant Navy and Liverpool's liner firms have been affected as much as anyone. Many fine cargo liners were sold off for trading under other flags. Some firms such as Ocean (Blue Funnel) no longer own any liners, while others have diversified into bulk carriers, tankers and accommodation vessels.

Today there are only a few cargo liners calling at Liverpool and none of them are Liverpool-owned.

This photograph of an unidentified Allan liner (Liverpool to Canada) is a reminder of just how much sail steamers carried even into the 1880s. It was partly a matter of economy, although compound engines had improved steamers' economy considerably, and partly a matter of having a propulsion system which would get the ship to a safe haven if there was trouble with a single propeller.

Trustees of NMGM

The White Star Liner *Teutonic* (1889) was a marked advance on the vessel of the previous picture with twin screws and a gross tonnage of almost double at 9,984 tons and without sails. She is at anchor in the river receiving coal supplies from Mersey sailing flats. She will also take her passengers on board in the same position. The water alongside the Landing Stage was not deep enough to berth large liners.

Trustees of NMGM

Major passenger liners increased rapidly in size after 1900. The White Star liner, with its competitor the Cunard, dominated the Liverpool transatlantic services. The *Adriatic* pictured in dry dock was built in 1907 and had a gross tonnage of 24,541 tons, a major increase in size again on the *Teutonic*. This type of new super-liner called for improved facilities in the port.

The Cunard liner *Mauretania* and her sister ship *Lusitania* of 1907, with a gross tonnage of 31,938, were the biggest, fastest, most innovative liners of their day. This amateur photograph captures the power and beauty of this famous liner alongside the Landing Stage in about 1910.

Trustees of NMGM

The fascination of *Mauretania* lives on. Models and relics from her, such as her brass stern letters, are still a potent attraction.

Trustees of NMGM

A second *Mauretania* was built at Cammell Laird's yard, Birkenhead in 1938 (*see also p. 88*). This photograph shows her in cruising colours in Gladstone Dock in 1963.

The White Star liner *Britannic* and her sister ship *Georgic* represented a further step in the development of the liner. They were diesel-engined vessels at a time when most ships including liners were driven by steam triple expansion engines or turbines.

In 1896 passenger facilities were greatly improved at Liverpool by building the Riverside station for boat trains and by making it possible for liners to come alongside the Landing Stage. This helped to combat the increasing competition from ports such as Southampton.

Trustees of NMGM

There were mobile gangways for passengers to pass easily undercover from the boat trains and waiting rooms of the ship. It was rather like the arrangement for boarding a modern 'jumbo' jet.

Williams Collection, Trustees of NMGM

Ratguards: there were also arrangements to prevent less welcome passengers getting on board.

Williams Collection, Trustees of NMGM

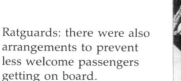

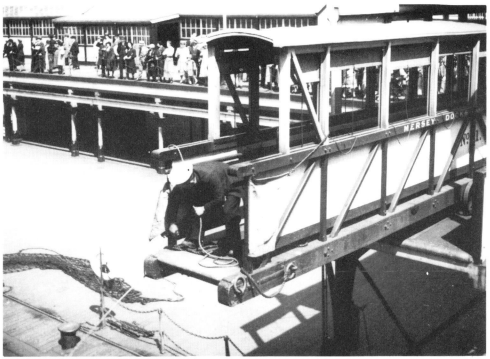

Sailing time – the Dock Board officials begin to retract the gangway and the last link with the shore.

The *Carinthia* blows her whistle to signal her departure on a cruise. Cruising was a useful source of income to passenger liner companies in the 1930s when the regular routes had surplus tonnage.

As the Landing Stage was so central to Liverpool, departures of liners such as the *Carinthia* were a great public spectacle and one that is sadly missed today.

The great steam windlass of the ship begins to turn to take in the mooring ropes.

The tugs take the strain and pull the huge ship sideways clear of the Landing Stage.

Williams Collection, Trustess of NMGM

The great ship, in this case, the *Britannic*, begins her voyage to America.

Williams Collection, Trustees of NMGM

Cargo carrying was a less glamorous side of liner traffic. Most great passenger liners spent some time in the North Docks to load and discharge cargo before going to the Landing Stage to collect their passengers.

MDHB Collection, Trustees of NMGM

Besides the passenger liners, there were many more cargo liners which also carried a few passengers. Few had such a dramatic arrival in the port approaches as the *Green Briar* in 1921. This remarkable photograph shows her in the act of hitting the Formby lightship.

MDHB Collection, Trustees of NMGM

The *Highland Chieftain* of the Nelson Line is shown in ballast and on trial for her makers Cammell Laird. She was part of an increasing trend after 1900 towards larger cargo liners and specialization. In her case, she was designed to carry refrigerated cargoes of meat from South America.

Trustees of NMGM

The Blue Funnel liner is glimpsed through the cargo handling gear of a ship in the foreground, showing the elaborate array of winches and derricks needed for cargo liners to offer an efficient service. Cargo had to be delivered to perhaps a dozen destinations on the outward voyage.

Williams Collection, Trustees of NMGM

Discharging cartons of tinned fruit. This photograph shows something of the size of the cargo liner and the labour intensive methods of handling goods once they had been landed.

A sign of the times: the Blue Funnel liner *Neleus* is towed from the West
Float at Birkenhead into Bidston Dock to be laid up. During the 1930s all
liner companies suffered from lack of trade. Some went out of business
and others, such as Cunard and White Star, had to merge in order to
survive.

MDHB Collection, Trustees of NMGM

This photograph of the cruising liner *Caronia* symbolizes the end of an
era. In 1967 the Cunard Line withdrew the last of its regular services
from Liverpool. The last liner of any company was Elder Dempster's
Aureol in 1971. After that, the future of deep-sea passenger liners was in
providing cruiser holidays. *Caronia* was something of a pioneer because
she was built purposely for this traffic in 1949.

Trustees of NMGM

The launch of the second *Mauretania* from Cammell Laird's yard in 1938, a great occasion on the Mersey.

MDHB Collection, Trustees of NMGM

Chapter Six

COASTERS, FERRIES AND TUGS

The first steamer on the Mersey was *Elizabeth* of 1815 plying between Liverpool and Runcorn. Two years later, a double-hulled craft, called the *Etna*, was built and engined at Liverpool for ferrying passengers and vehicles from South Ferry Basin, Liverpool, to Tranmere. Despite problems of mechanical reliability, (the *Elizabeth*, for example, was converted from steam to horsepower in 1818), ferry steamers for the cross-river passage were in regular use in the 1820s and by 1829 there were steamers coastwise and across the Irish sea: to Bagillt, Beaumaris, Belfast, Bangor, Bristol, Cork, Drogheda, Dublin, Glasgow, the Isle of Man, Lancaster, Newry, Londonderry, Wexford and Whitehaven. Steamers provided a hitherto unheard of regularity of service for passengers and small parcels of goods. The passage across the Mersey under sail could take hours in bad weather and days across the Irish Sea. The paddle-steamer *Mona* on the Liverpool–Dublin run averaged about twenty hours for the passage and at worst thirty-seven. She carried passengers, and occasionally freight, and frequently set sails to assist the engines.

Ferry services across the Mersey also helped to make possible the development of a new town on the Wallasey Pool, Birkenhead, a new class of businessman commuter who set up his home on the rural Wirral and worked in Liverpool, and a pleasure resort for sea bathing at New Brighton. The developers and the ferryowners were often the same people. Sir John Tobin, John Askew and the harbour master of Liverpool had a substantial stake in house building at Egremont and in the connecting ferry company. It was not surprising that many of the early steamers were tugs for the Mersey – the river was notoriously difficult to enter under sail; and ferries would also go seeking lucrative towing work to the annoyance of the passengers.

By 1858, however, ferries and tugs were distinct classes of vessels owned by different companies. After the first three decades of glorious private enterprise, local government in the form of Birkenhead Commissioners took charge of the ferry to Woodside and later others within their district. Similarly, in 1862 the Wallasey Commissioners took charge of the Seacombe service and later the New Brighton and Egremont services; and the red and black funnels of the Birkenhead boats and the white and black of the Wallasey fleet became an enduring feature of the river scene. Landing arrangements were also considerably improved by the construction of floating landing stages – the first being George's stage in 1847. Vehicles were carried on specially designed ferries which were nicknamed 'luggage boats'. The ferries attracted competition first with the Mersey railway, completed at vast cost in 1889, and then after 1900, with the construction of electric tramways connecting with this underground railway. The opening of the first road tunnel in 1934 also took away traffic. The more distant, less patronized ferries were closed one by one. Today, the Wirral has only two ferry terminals at Seacombe and Woodside and for a large part of the day the ferries run trips for tourists.

The railways had a significant impact on coastal services particularly on the North Wales services, which had become mainly summer excursion services by the 1880s. Messrs Powell and Hough provided passenger cabins on their services to Bristol, London and Glasgow, up to the 1920s; but the voyages were for pleasure, not necessity and the regular service was basically for goods. Liverpool had several rival ports to Ireland, particularly Holyhead, which had the shortest crossing to Kingstown and Dublin. Nevertheless, regular passenger and freight services grew rapidly and more and larger iron-hulled vessels were built. The export of cattle from Ireland grew to a spectacular scale and by 1900 such was its volume that there were special landing stages at Woodside and Wallasey close to the lairages. Paddles, with their superior manoeuvring ability, remained the most popular means of propulsion for passenger vessels until the development of twin screw steamers. The last paddlers were very spectacular indeed; the Isle of Man Steam Packet Company's *Empress Queen* of 1897 could steam at 22 knots and carry over 2,000 day passengers.

While the regular coastal liners carried considerable quantities of foodstuffs and manufactures from an early date, bulk carrying by steam was a relatively late development. The first important step was probably the carriage of salt by steam barges down the Weaver to Liverpool in 1864, although steam tugs hauling dumb flats had been introduced on the Mersey and Irwell as early as 1832. The Weaver steamers known as 'packets' had their engines right aft to provide one large clear hold for ease of cargo handling. They also towed up to three dumb barges; such a combination proved very economical with the flotilla carrying something in the region of one thousand tons of salt.

Coasters were designed with a similar layout, engines

and bridge aft, and a long single hold with single mast forward and a derrick for working the cargo. Later versions had a bridge placed at the forward end of a raised quarter deck. Diesel power was a possibility from the 1930s but was initially more common among the British coasters' main rivals, the Dutch. Cargoes carried were the same as the schooners although some companies had specialities such as the summer vegetable-fruit-carrying charters from the Channel Islands. There were others specializing in coal-carrying to Ireland. Coastal tankers for oil and a wide range of chemicals and other liquids carried in bulk, including the famous Guinness stout, became a very important feature of the port's coastal traffic. Today, for example, there is a daily procession of small oil and chemical tankers up the Mersey to the refineries of the Manchester Ship Canal.

Tugs continue a vital role in moving large ships in and out of the docks. The first ones were paddle tugs which were highly manoeuvrable but not very powerful. By 1900, screw-propelled tugs had become the norm with towage controlled by a few large companies. Steam engines were retained until the mid-1960s because of their ruggedness and reliability. Clean air legislation helped to force owners to change over to diesels.

Today's tugs are as powerful as earlier generations of ocean-going tugs and the most modern are fitted with special propulsion systems that make them even more manoeuvrable than the old paddlers. Nevertheless, the skill and judgement of the tugmaster still remains of paramount importance, especially because the deep-sea ships have grown so much in size. Two Mersey steam tugs have been preserved: the *Canning* at Swansea Maritime Museum and the barge tug *Kerne* which still steams on the River Mersey in summer despite being launched in 1913.

The Isle of Man Steam Packet Company, founded in 1830, is one of the oldest established coastal liner firms. The turbine steamer *Mona's Queen* approaches the Landing Stage in 1951.

Williams Collection, Trustees of NMGM

The *Mona's Queen* docking at the Landing Stage.

Williams Collection, Trustees of NMGM

The *Manx Maid* at the Landing Stage in 1947, looking for all the world like a miniature liner.

Williams Collection, Trustees of NMGM

An earlier *Manx Maid* demonstrates with her canvas side screens just how stormy the waters of the Irish Sea can be. A Royal Mail lorry can be seen delivering the Manx post in the bottom right corner.

Williams Collection, Trustees of NMGM

The first *Manxman* was a turbine steamer built for the Midland Railway Company Service from Heysham and acquired by the Isle of Man company in 1920. This photograph gives an impression of her speed.

Williams Collection, Trustees of NMGM

Liverpool maintained coastal services with the Irish mainland from an early date. The steamer *Kenmare* is pictured here departing for Cork.

Williams Collection, Trustees of NMGM

The Dublin boat *Munster* in 1938 in Prince's Dock. This splendid vessel hit a mine and sank in 1939.

Williams Collection, Trustees of NMGM

The Belfast boat *Ulster Monarch* is clearly from the same shipyard as the *Britannic*.

Landing Irish cattle at Woodside landing stage, 1923.

MDHB Collection, Trustees of NMGM

'I remember the good old days'. Two of the crew of the Isle of Man steam turbine ship *Manxman* reminisce on her last voyage in 1982.

Hibernian Coast was one of the large fleet of Coast Lines which amounted to over a hundred vessels at its high point. Services for cargo and twelve passengers sailed from Liverpool to most major British ports.

What appears to be a typical steam coaster with bridge amidships is in fact the pioneer motor ship *Fullagar*, the first all welded vessel in the world, built at Laird's yard in 1920.

Trustees of NMGM

Most coasters were unpretentious bulk carriers. The *Barrule* was a Second World War pre-fabricated coaster of standard design and almost attractive in its ugliness.

Williams Collection, Trustees of NMGM

Coal was the major coastal traffic and this collier from Garston is seen outward bound on the sunlit waters of the Mersey.

Williams Collection, Trustees of NMGM

Waiting for the ferry about 1890.

Williams Collection, Trustees of NMGM

The forerunner of the famous New Brighton landing stage and pier was primitive but had the beginnings of providing an excursion place for Merseysiders. Note the refreshment room in the foreground.

Trustees of NMGM

Crowded paddle ferry, the *Gem*, leaves New Brighton in 1865 amid inward bound sailing vessels.

Trustees of NMGM

THE FERRY, ROCK FERRY

Rock Ferry terminal. The Mersey ferries also provided access for middle class commuters living in the new suburbs of the Wirral. This picture is of the rural tranquility where today there is a major oil terminal.

Trustees of NMGM

The ferries also provided vehicle transport until the opening of the Mersey tunnel. This picture shows one of the luggage boats laden with horse-drawn wagons bound for Birkenhead.

Williams Collection, Trustees of NMGM

Steam tug *North Rock* in Brunswick Dock gives a good impression of the power of the steam tug.

Williams Collection, Trustees of NMGM

Two tugs at work docking a cargo liner.

Williams Collection, Trustees of NMGM

The *Alexandra*
manoeuvres a
passenger liner
through the narrow
Sandon entrance at
high tide. Towage was
a skilful business.

Williams Collection,
Trustees of NMGM

Almost at sea a motor tug *Herculaneum* swings the bow of the *Pacific Envoy*.

Tugs were also used to tow flats and other barges around the docks and to upriver destinations.

The tug skippers of the Cock Towing Company who were to take charge of the aircraft carrier *Ark Royal* when launched from Cammell Laird's yard.

Alexandra Towing Company

Chapter Seven

YACHTS AND PADDLERS

Looking at the greasy, polluted waters of the Mersey of today ringed with the chimneys of industry, it is difficult to imagine our ancestors bathing in its clear water at long-gone resorts like Bootle, or relaxing among the wooded groves of the Dingle. Much of the shoreline close to Liverpool was used for extensions to the dock system; Bootle's sands went to build Canada Dock in the 1850s; and the Dingle at the southern end of the city disappeared under oil tanks in the 1930s; other industrial projects such as the Manchester Ship Canal and the extension of Laird's shipyard into Tranmere, helped erode the natural beauty and attraction of the estuary. Furthermore, with the increased availability of convenient forms of travel by road and rail, and improved holidays and incomes, the river and its resorts have since declined in popularity though sailing still flourishes.

In 1858, the river was a great attraction to both the wealthy and poor of Liverpool alike, and while the rich man might take to his yacht, the steam ferries to Eastham and New Brighton, or a day excursion to North Wales provided a welcome change from the dirty, downcast streets of the city slums.

The first organized regatta on the Mersey was recorded

as 1828. The first Mersey Yacht Club was formed in 1844 by sixteen leading members of commerce and shipping. The following year the club received royal patronage. In return members were expected to escort visiting members of the royal family both in and out of port, wearing, of course, the club uniform – a kind of formality that contrasts with the informality of most of today's clubs. In 1846 Prince Albert visited the club. Two years later the Commodore, Harold Littledale, in his yacht, *Queen of the Ocean*, saved many people from the emigrant ship *Ocean Monarch* which caught fire in Liverpool Bay. The *Queen of the Ocean* was a typical specimen of the club's yachts – a heavily rigged cutter with long bowsprit and jackyard topsail, more suited for cruising and offshore racing than sailing in the crowded river.

A second club was founded in 1869, and this one, the New Brighton Sailing Club, was formed for sailing open boats on the river itself. In the 1870s they developed a twenty-three-foot boat rigged with huge, balanced lug mainsail, mizzen and long bowsprit, heavily ballasted and crewed by six men, three of whom were carried as mobile ballast.

Sailing canoes came into fashion in the 1860s; the Mersey canoe was usually about seventeen feet long, clinker-built with balanced lug mainsail and mizzen, fitted with a centreboard and was raced by the local canoe club. The canoes were the direct predecessors of the sailing dinghies that came into fashion in the 1900s, for example the gunter-rigged sixteen foot 'West Kirby Star' class started in 1909.

Despite the problems of sailing on a busy and dangerous river, nearly a dozen clubs were racing on the Mersey and in Liverpool Bay in 1914. This prosperous state was cut short by the First World War, and some clubs wound up their affairs in the 1920s. Those that survived continued to keep abreast of contemporary developments in yacht design and notably, in this post-war period, the Royal Mersey Yacht Club introduced a new Mylne-designed class of three-quarter-decked dayboats with Bermudan rig.

Eastham Ferry, upstream from Liverpool on the Cheshire bank of the Mersey, was a popular finishing point for many of the early races, until it became too commercialized for the middle class yachtsmen. As the historian of the Royal Mersey Yacht Club wrote: 'Eastham, in those days, was justly named the Richmond of the Mersey: there were miles of forest carpeted with flowers and bracken, all free and open. There was then no fenced in trippers' paradise with its miserable zoo, rowdy booths, merry-go-rounds and ham and egg parade. A rural hotel and two or three refreshment rooms among the strawberry gardens there were, and a picnic at Eastham was quite an aristocratic function.' As the writer suggests, the growth of cheap steam ferry services in the 1840s and '50s encouraged the less well-off of Liverpool and the Lancashire industrial towns to go on day excursions to Eastham, New Brighton and even to North Wales and the Isle of Man; for example, as early as 1863, the Isle of Man Steam Packet Company were running trips to the Isle of Man which connected with excursion trains from inland towns to Liverpool.

New Brighton, at the mouth of the Mersey, was intended to be a select bathing resort (as the name implied) in 1833 when James Atherton established a ferry service, a hotel, and began building seaside villas on 170 acres of land. Like Eastham, it became generally popular and many other amusements were introduced to cater for popular tastes. By 1898, there was a fun-fair and an

Eiffel-type, wrought iron tower taller than its rival at Blackpool.

North Wales was a popular choice for an excursion and for some a holiday in the late nineteenth century for a return ticket could cost as little as five shillings and sixpence. Such was the demand for summer excursions that the two companies competing from Liverpool carried nearly a quarter of a million people between May and September 1891 in three steamers. In the same year, these rivals, the New North Wales Steamship Company and the Liverpool Llandudno and Welsh Coast Steam Boat Company (the successor to the Welsh Coast services that started in the 1820s), merged to form the Liverpool and North Wales Steam Ship Company which specialized in summer excursions from Liverpool to Llandudno, Menai Bridge etc., with a fleet of fast paddle-steamers. The company's *La Marguerite* paddle-steamer, purchased in 1904, was one of the most well-known ships on the river. She was replaced in 1926 by two large twin screw turbine steamers, which were as popular as their predecessors. But the river resorts declined after the First World War: Eastham lost its ferry service in 1929 and New Brighton scrapped its imposing tower.

The waterfront of the port held many pleasures too; the Overhead railway, opened in 1892, was a popular excursion because of its splendid view of the docks and the closeness of its northern terminus to the sands of Seaforth and Crosby. On the dock road, and up many neighbouring side streets, there were pubs, bars, brothels and music halls. The night-life of Liverpool's 'sailortown' was notorious, even in 1900, though by local tradition it enjoyed its finest hours in the rip-roaring years of the 1850s and '60s.

The queen of the North Wales day excursion steamers, *La Marguerite*, sails for Llandudno.

Messing about with a boat. Children paddling at New Brighton, 1910.

Trustees of NMGM

Canal-side fishing, about 1900.

Williams Collection, Trustees of NMGM

Carrying out running repairs aboard a large sailing yacht.

Trustees of NMGM

Dismasted. Races on the Mersey were keenly contested and sometimes masts and gear did not carry the strain.

Williams Collection, Trustees of NMGM

The luxury yacht *Sea Cloud* pays a call to the Mersey. She is still afloat today with a full rig as a cruise liner.

Williams Collection, Trustees of NMGM

The Royal Mersey Yacht Club race. Founded in 1844, the Royal Mersey was the doyen of the local sailing clubs with an anchorage and large clubhouse at Tranmere.

Williams Collection, Trustees of NMGM

Sailing yachts is not just a wealthy man's pastime thanks to organizations like the Ocean Youth Club. Here, two of their fine seventy-foot boats are seen on the Mersey in 1980.

Trustees of NMGM

Chapter Eight
LIGHTHOUSES, LIGHTSHIPS AND SERVICE VESSELS

The entrance and passage of the Mersey were extremely difficult to navigate under sail with the hazards of rapid tides and shifting channels between treacherous sandbanks. As the number of ships trading to Liverpool increased, so the need for services for conservancy and safe navigation increased. By 1858 these services were numerous and complex. Sea and landmarks, surveying, pilotage, dredging, salvage and life-saving services provided a safe passage from the outer approaches off Point Lynas, Anglesey, across the Mersey Bar and into the river.

Unlit landmarks were the first navigational aids; there was a long established perch or marker on the rocks where the New Brighton Lighthouse now stands. From 1762 there was an extensive programme of lighthouse building, firstly to mark the two ends of the Hoyle Lake anchorage and followed by a whole network of lights and marks, at Bidston, Point of Ayr, Point Lynas, Formby and Bootle. Buoys were anchored to mark the limits of the main channels, and in 1813 the first lightship was moored at what became known as the North-West station; later, three more lightships were stationed at strategic positions along the main channel (Formby lightship 1834, Crosby

1840 and the Bar 1873). Improvements to buoys, such as equipping them with bells and flashing lights lit by acetylene, culminated in the construction of unmanned boat beacons in the 1920s to replace all the lightships except the Bar lightship.

Conservancy and surveying assumed a vital importance as the size and therefore the draught of vessels increased. A number of detailed charts had been drawn up in the eighteenth century, but revision and updating never kept pace with the movements of sandbanks and channels. The Dock Trustees of the 1820s commissioned experienced naval hydrographers, like Denham and Lord, who pinpointed the exact position of the deep-water Queen's Channel, and their efforts led to the formation of a regular surveying department under the Dock Board carrying out monthly and annual surveys and publishing its own charts.

Positive improvements by removing large quantities of silt were made possible by the application of the steam engine to dredging. A steam bucket dredger started work in the docks in about 1826. In the first years of Birkenhead Docks in the 1840s, a method of sluicing away the silt was tried and abandoned because the miniature tidal wave released endangered the ships in port. As the dock system grew so the fleet of dredgers increased, with both bucket, ladder and grab dredgers and their attendant hopper barges constantly at work to keep the docks and their entrances open. However, the main channel and the Bar was subject to silting without remedy and by the 1880s the lack of water on the Bar at low tide was a constant grumble by the larger liner owners. In 1890 two hopper barges were converted into suction dredgers. Long trailing tubes enabled them to clear silt to a much greater depth than the other types of dredger and their success was considerable.

They were able to cut a deep channel through the Bar, giving twenty-five feet of water at low tide as against the previous eleven. Specially constructed suction dredgers were constantly employed to deepen and keep clear the approach channel. In 1906 work started on building stone revetments on either side of the channel to stabilize its route.

The pilotage service was first established on a regular system in 1766, with licensed pilots from regular stations. The pilots continued to own their boats and administer their own affairs until 1881. The original pilot boats were small cutters, but these were replaced by twelve very seaworthy schooners, the first of which went into service in 1852. In 1896 steam pilot cutters replaced the schooners, but the traditions of a very skilled, very hazardous profession were carried on.

Despite the many precautions to ensure the safe passage of shipping to and from the Mersey, wrecks, collisions and other casualties still occurred. About 1771 the Dock Trust organized the first lifeboat service, which eventually provided stations for sailing and pulling lifeboats at strategic points – Hilbre Island, Hoylake, Point of Ayr, the Magazines, the Pier Head and Formby. Salvage or the removal of wrecks was another responsibility. Under the Dock Board, the salvage section of the engineer's department had a fleet of wreck-marking vessels, lifting camels and salvage craft to remove navigational hazards as quickly as possible. These salvage problems, both in the river and the docks (where fire was a particular hazard) were recorded in detail by the board's own photographers, reflecting the importance of removing, as quickly as possible, any interruptions in the flow of ships.

New Brighton lighthouse at low tide marks the end of the Wirral peninsula and its prominent red sandstone rocks.

Trustees of NMGM

The Bar lightship *Planet* is towed back to her station by the buoy tender *Salvor*. She once marked the beginning of the Mersey approach channel.

Williams Collection, Trustees of NMGM

From the Bar, the main channel was marked on either side by distinctive buoys. C19 is one from the Crosby channel and is about to be lifted from its mooring on to the deck of the *Salvor*.

The Liverpool pilot service has provided expert advice for vessels using the difficult Mersey estuary. *William H. Clarke*, built in 1937, was the last of the steam vessels.

The introduction of trailing suction dredging made it possible to deepen the Bar and the approaches to the river. This picture shows the *Tulip* working to deepen the water off the New Brighton landing stage.

Trustees of NMGM

The maintenance of the approach channel was a major expense and a fleet of dredgers and hopper barges were kept in constant use. This picture shows Number 12 outward bound with a load of silt for dumping beyond the Bar about 1936.

Williams Collection, Trustees of NMGM

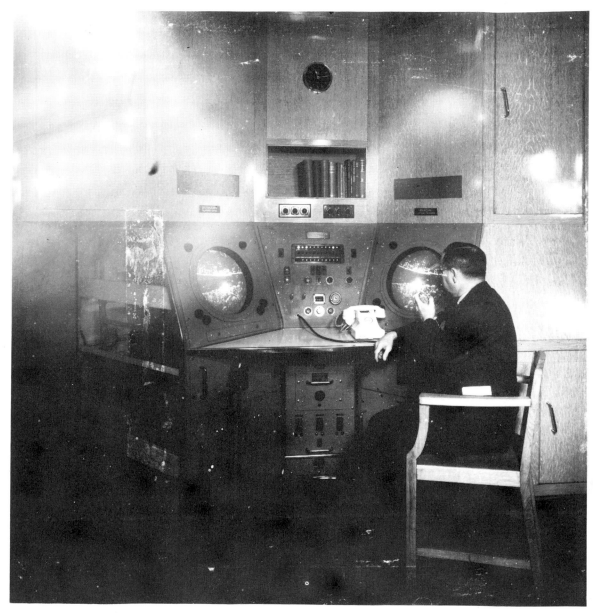

The port was the first to set up radar equipment to monitor ships entering and leaving. This photograph shows the original 1948 console which is today preserved at the Science Museum in London.

Stewart Bale, Trustees of NMGM

The Dock Board ran a flotilla of floating cranes for heavy lifts including the Mammoth, the biggest in the world, shown here lifting a new bridge for the New Brighton ferry stage in 1920.

Trustees of NMGM

In spite of other well-marked channels and expert pilots, accidents and collisions did occasionally occur. Liverpool and Glasgow Salvage Association maintained the *Ranger*, an old Victorian ex-gun-boat, as a salvage steamer until 1954. She is seen here at her usual base in Albert Dock with a number of other Dock Board service vessels.

Williams Collection, Trustees of NMGM

The wooden steamer *Veritas* was run down by a larger steamer off New Brighton. Abandoned by her crew she drifted derelict upriver to become entangled with the booms of the Landing Stage. It was a difficult operation in 1900 for the Dock Board salvage crew to extract and refloat her.

Trustees of NMGM

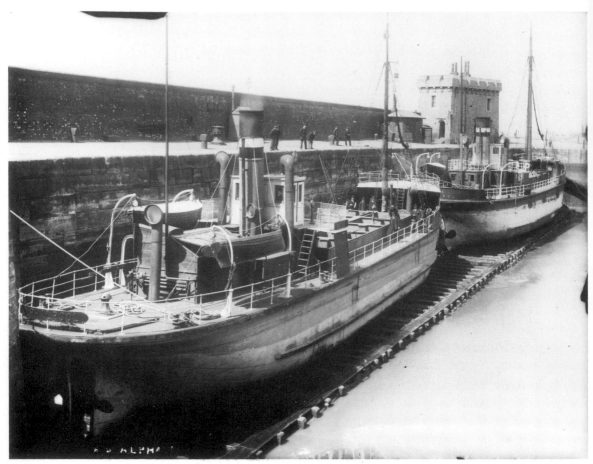

Although it may sound incredible in these days of green consciousness, all the domestic refuse from Liverpool was once dumped at sea by hopper barges such as the *Alpha* and the *Delta* seen at Clarence Dock in this picture.

Liverpool City Engineers

Two Dock Board salvage camels for lifting sunken wrecks laid up with other craft in Albert Dock including the tender *Galatea* (*left*) and a fishing nobby (*foreground*).

Chapter Nine

COASTAL SCHOONERS

Before the 1830s and the spread of railways and steamers, sailing craft had been the main method of distribution between Liverpool and the inland towns of the Mersey, and the waterways connecting with the Mersey, North Wales, the Isle of Man and Ireland. Regular packet services for passengers and goods – for example shop-keepers' supplies – were the waterborne equivalent of the local carrier on the roads. Two types of carrying had all but ceased by 1858 and the work of coastal sailing craft was mainly in carrying raw materials in bulk: coal from the Lancashire mines for Liverpool or for export, salt from Cheshire, china clay from Cornwall to Runcorn for the Staffordshire potteries, iron ore and pig iron from the mines and blast furnaces of Furness, and stone from North Wales.

Leaving aside fishing boats and pilot schooners, most coastal sailing craft were schooners trading to the ports all around the Irish Sea. Fleets of schooners were owned in the smaller ports around Liverpool, Runcorn, Connah's Quay (on the Dee) and Barrow being noted centres.

By 1850, the schooner rig with square topsails on the foremast seemed to be growing in popularity for the coasting trade in and out of the Mersey. The rig was both more economical in terms of manpower, requiring only four to six in a crew as against seven or more for a brig or brigantine, and more manoeuvrable in confined waters.

Hundreds of schooners were involved in the china clay trade to Runcorn and the coal trade at Garston.

Schooners were built on the Mersey, not so many in the Liverpool yards which tended to concentrate on iron and steel deep-water vessels, but at Runcorn and Widnes. They were also built on the Dee at Connah's Quay, at Freckleton on the Ribble, at Fleetwood, Ulverston and Barrow, and in fact all the schooners of the North West were known to the West Country centres of schooners – ports such as Appledore and Barnstaple – as 'Barrow Flats'. The nickname emphasized their common characteristics: little change in draught fore and aft (unlike the Devon and Cornish vessels), flat floors to take ground and remain upright at low tide, an ability to sail with little or no ballast, great handiness in sailing in narrow waters, and commonly a pointed stern with the rudder hung outboard. The best of their type were very strongly built and a fair number of these stout vessels continued trading (with auxiliary engines) well into the 1950s.

Iron- and steel-hulled schooners were not built until the mid-1880s, and by this time they were facing increasing competition from steam powered coasters.

Cargo capacities of coastal sailing ships varied from about 100 tons to up to 300 – quite small compared with most of the steamers but suitable for the small cargoes on offer in the small ports of the Irish Sea. Cargoes carried were generally raw materials in bulk; for example, in 1884, the *James Postlethwaite* carried coal, bricks, cement, timber, stone, manure, china clay and pitwood. Cement demanding a dry tight ship offered the best return at 9s per ton, while coal and china clay averaged between 3s and 3s 6d. Even in those non-inflationary days, this was not much return when set against all the running expenses of the vessel and the crew's wages. None the less there was a widespread ownership of shares in schooners among the small shipping communities such as the upriver port of Runcorn.

The two main centres for coastal sail on the Mersey were Runcorn and Garston. Runcorn had its own fleet of vessels, many of which had been built locally. Many more schooners from other ports were always in dock, mainly delivering china clay from Cornwall. Even in 1900 when the steam coasters were bringing in china clay, Runcorn averaged about thirty schooner arrivals every month. A fleet of schooners bound out of the Mersey was one of the most memorable sights on the river. Garston was a port developed by the railways for coal shipments from the Lancashire coal fields and many schooners were loaded under the coal tips of Garston for the Irish ports or elsewhere. The last schooner to trade on the river was the Irish-owned *De Wadden* who carried her last coal cargo in about 1960. Today she is being preserved at the Merseyside Maritime Museum.

Schooner *My Lady of Plymouth* running before the wind.

David Smith Collection, Liverpool Nautical Research Society

Mabel of Barrow close-hauled after leaving Canning Half-Tide entrance in 1924.

David Smith Collection, Liverpool Nautical Research Society

The ex-fruit schooner *Via* inward bound with a cargo of stone in 1931.

David Smith Collection, Liverpool Nautical Research Society

The *Emma* and *Esther* under tow.

David Smith Collection, Liverpool Nautical Research Society

Discharging a cargo in the traditional way with a hand winch.

Trustees of NMGM

Racing past the Liver Buildings.

David Smith Collection, Liverpool Nautical Research Society

Unknown Dutch schooner outward bound.

David Smith Collection, Liverpool Nautical Research Society

Under full sail passing the last luggage steamer, the *Perch Rock*.

David Smith Collection, Liverpool Nautical Research Society

The sole survivor, the *De Wadden*, of 1917, was bought for preservation in 1984 by Merseyside Maritime Museum. This picture shows her on one of her last voyages to Garston for coal in the 1950s.

Trustees of NMGM

Shipwrecked, the schooner *Creek Fisher* ashore at Blundellsands off the river entrance in 1916.

Trustees of NMGM

Chapter Ten
THE ROYAL NAVY

Liverpool, though never a naval base, was always of importance to the Royal Navy. Its shipyards built warships, it was a good recruiting ground, and a port for the showing of the flag in peace time and for protection in war.

Liverpool's eighteenth-century shipbuilders received occasional orders for frigates and sloops from the navy, including the 40-gun HMS *Liverpool*, launched in 1741, and after 1840 Laird's of Birkenhead became an important supplier of warships, both to the Royal Navy and foreign powers including the Confederate States during the American Civil War. They began their naval connection with the construction of HMS *Dover*, the first iron warship. Laird's also built HMS *Captain*, a revolutionary design of turret ship which capsized on exercises in 1870. Her loss, although through no fault of the builders, put Laird's out of Admiralty favour for almost a decade. But in the late 1880s they were building battleships and the new class of warship – the torpedo-boat destroyer. During the First World War, the yard undertook the building of a large number of warships including submarines (the first in 1915), plus the repair of warships and the conversion of merchant ships for wartime roles. Laird's have continued to secure important naval orders, for example, the battleship HMS *Rodney* in 1927, and even today their staple work is for the Royal Navy.

Liverpool's many eighteenth-century seamen attracted repeated visits of press-gangs, while in the nineteenth century more peaceable forms of recruitment included the establishment of a Royal Naval Reserve depot on board an old wooden warship in Kings Dock, HMS *Eagle* (later *Eaglet*).

A squadron of four old wooden warships moored on the river housed and educated (and in the case of *Akbar* and *Clarence* 'reformed') boys – orphaned, delinquent and those destined to be merchant navy officers (HMS *Conway*). The vessels were commanded by naval officers on half-pay and were run on very naval lines. These establishments were eventually all moved ashore as their old hulks deteriorated. Only HMS *Conway* was left by the 1930s.

Visits by single naval vessels to show the flag were a frequent occurrence, and on a few memorable occasions, a whole fleet could be seen in port. In August 1888 a squadron of nineteen vessels attacked and captured the port, which had been defended by a second and much smaller squadron. In August 1907 probably the largest fleet ever to visit Liverpool arrived, led by HMS *King Edward VII*, supported by seventeen other battleships and cruisers. Such naval spectaculars naturally attracted the photographer.

From the early nineteenth century, Liverpool had been protected by gun batteries at the mouth of the Mersey. The New Brighton fort still survives, but the Seaforth battery, the last of a succession of forts on the northern bank, was removed for the Gladstone Dock. Bombardment by enemy vessels in Liverpool Bay remained a real fear even in the First World War.

From the 1880s the Dock Board, the shipowners and the Admiralty had drawn up agreements to protect the port and make use of fast liners as armed merchant cruisers in time of war. Measures were to include the removal of navigation marks and the extinguishing of lighthouses and were carried out on the outbreak of the First World War. Although Liverpool was never directly attacked, the port facilities were under severe strain with the diversion of ships from other ports, shortage of men, lack of maintenance, and the need to reconcile military requirements with those of commerce.

Liverpool ships served with distinction: for example the armed merchant cruiser *Carmania*, which sank her German equivalent, the *Cap Trafalgar* in 1914, and the two gallant Mersey ferry steamers, the *Royal Iris* and the *Royal Daffodil* which took part in the Zeebrugge Raid in 1917.

The port was in the front line in the Second World War. Convoys of merchant ships bearing vital supplies from America docked and assembled in the Mersey. Liverpool housed the headquarters of Western Approaches Command and a whole range of associated naval establishments, together with bases for escorts and minesweepers in the Gladstone and Birkenhead Docks. The port was badly damaged in bombing attacks, especially in the great raids of May 1941. But in spite of the damage the port never stopped working.

The links with the navy continue. Visiting warships always receive a warm welcome and there is a permanent though small naval presence in the shape of the Royal Navy's regional office and the Royal Naval Reserve depot, HMS *Eaglet*.

The navy's peacetime presence in the port is maintained by the Royal Naval Reserve. The old wooden warship, HMS *Eagle*, looking rather like Noah's Ark, was the base until 1927.

Trustees of NMGM

HMS *Sans Pareil* at anchor off the Pier Head about 1890–1945. Visiting warships have always attracted attention in Liverpool.

Trustees of NMGM

Four other ex-wooden sailing warships provided training ships for young seafarers. These 'boarding schools' were moored in Tranmere and provided a tough introduction to the joys of the sea.

Trustees of NMGM

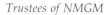

This squadron of minesweepers seen in Albert Dock in 1936 are very similar to the escort vessels that were based in the port to protect the convoys of merchant men plying the Atlantic. Liverpool was the central port for the Battle of the Atlantic. Albert Dock provided one base for escort vessels.

Trustees of NMGM

Warships have been built on the Mersey since the eighteenth century.
Perhaps the three most notable ones are the battleship *Rodney* of 1927,
and two aircraft carriers called *Ark Royal*.

This picture shows the second *Ark Royal* after launching, being towed into Cammell Laird's fitting-out basin for completion in 1950.

Trustees of NMGM

The most prestigious naval vessel, the Royal Yacht *Britannia*, leaves the Landing Stage in 1958.

Merchantman turned warship. The Cunard liner *Campania* (1892) found a new role in the First World War as an aircraft carrier. She was converted at Cammell Laird's yard and given a platform over her bow for launching sea planes. The two derricks on either side of her bridge were for recovering them after they had landed in the water. Note the later Cunard liner, *Mauretania*, in the background of this picture.

Trustees of NMGM

Many merchant ships were damaged by mines and torpedoes in both world wars and this picture shows two coastal vessels being repaired in Canning Graving Dock. Note the dazzle camouflage on their hulls. This was designed to break up their silhouette and make them more difficult to spot at sea.

Trustees of NMGM

In the Second World War enemy bombers attacked the port and caused great damage, particularly in the 1941 raids. However, it was never entirely put out of action. This shows Brunswick Dock with damaged transit sheds and the burnt out workshops of the Dock Board. In the background a convoy of ships at anchor.

Trustees of NMGM

Chapter Eleven

TANKERS AND CONTAINER SHIPS

The first specialist tanker for conveying oil in bulk was launched in 1886. By 1890 one Liverpool shipowning firm, H.E. Moss, had bought its first oil tanker. Tankers were to become an important part of the traffic of the port as demand for imported oil increased. Storage tanks were provided at the southern end of the docks in 1920. The growth of refineries on the banks of the Manchester Ship Canal increased the demand for oil handling facilities so much that a second terminal was added at Tranmere in 1960. This was designed to handle the rapidly increasing size of tankers. When first built, a large tanker could carry about 50,000 tons. Today, the terminal can handle ships of up to about 150,000 tons, the largest ships by far to enter the Mersey. Tankers have led the way to the more specialized ships of today. Cargo liners and tramp steamers, that is ships not on a regular service but 'tramping' from one voyage and one cargo to another, carried a wide variety of goods. Now bulk low cost cargoes such as coal or grain are carried in large bulk carriers or 'bulkers' which look very similar to tankers with their low profile, no cargo gear and high superstructure aft. Mixed cargo carried in 'break bulk' form is almost a thing of the past because all valuable cargo is containerized except where port facilities do not exist to handle the containers. Instead of carefully storing a mixed bag of goods in open holds, the specialized container ship has a grid of slots in which standard size steel boxes can be fitted. Once the hatches are closed another two or three tiers can be added on deck. The container can travel in the ship and also on a lorry trailer or railway wagon. It can be unloaded by a special container crane and thus the whole process of loading and unloading can be speeded up. A container ship may spend no more than twelve hours in Royal Seaforth Dock. The containers are taken away to be unpacked (or packed) at inland destinations. Similarly, wheeled cargo such as cars and trailers can be moved in and out of roll-on/roll-off ships by means of huge water-tight doors and lowering ramps at the bow and stern of the ship. Again, the speed of cargo handling is much improved. Both these innovations have revolutionized shipping. The container users of Royal Seaforth Dock make a distinctive contribution to the landscape of the port.

The Eagle Oil tanker *San Castro* in the ship canal. Although the Liverpool Docks had some provision for oil traffic at Herculaneum and Dingle, much of the oil business went up to the Manchester Ship Canal directly to the refineries at Stanlow.

Trustees of NMGM

As tankers began to increase rapidly in size in the late 1950s, a major new river terminal was built at Tranmere on the site of the old landing stage at Rock Ferry. A second jetty was erected as a tank cleaning berth; a Shell tanker is berthed alongside in this picture.

Trustees of NMGM

It is sometimes difficult to appreciate the size of modern tankers. This view shows what would now be considered to be the deck of a relatively small tanker, about 50,000 tons, in dry dock at Woodside, Birkenhead. Its size can be appreciated from the men working on deck.

Trustees of NMGM

This odd structure is the semi-submersible oil drilling platform *Sovereign Explorer* built at Cammell Laird's yard. She is being towed out to sea by five tugs.

Alexandra Towing Company

Aerial view of Royal Seaforth Docks opened in 1974. It was capable of receiving ships of up to 75,000 tons. Note the vast amount of space required for stacking containers in the modern container port.

Mersey Docks and Harbour Company

A close-up view of the container berth at Royal Seaforth Dock with three large ocean-going vessels being worked. The huge cranes lift the steel containers off the decks and out of the holds of the ships; the Atlantic compass in the foreground also has a lifting sternbridge for wheeled-cargoes such as cars for export. This 35,000-ton vessel can be loaded and discharged in a matter of about twelve hours.

Mersey Docks and Harbour Company

The grain terminal at Royal Seaforth Dock is one of the most modern in the world and can hold about 100,000 tons. Two large tower elevators are discharging the bulk carrier on the left, while the smaller vessel on the right is probably loading up grain for export.

Mersey Docks and Harbour Company

Royal Seaforth Dock at night. This picture shows a large stacker delivering a container to the quayside crane for loading on board ship.

Mersey Docks and Harbour Company

Royal Seaforth is also a major centre for the timber trade and this photograph shows two large timber ships with packaged timber as opposed to the old way of carrying it loose in individual pieces.

Mersey Docks and Harbour Company